Dedication

Chapter 1: Training 4 Victory

Chapter 2: No Competition

Chapter 3: Under New Management

Chapter 4: Weathering the Storm

Chapter 5: 100% Guaranteed

Chapter 6: Walking In Confidence (W.I.C)

Chapter 7: The Love of Christ (TLC)

Chapter 8: Conflict between Flesh & Spirit

Chapter 9: Knowing the Truth/Rejecting the False

Chapter 10: B.I.G (Believing In God)

Chapter 11: Understanding the Love of Christ

Chapter 12: Seek First; Everything else second

Chapter 13: True Holiness is Reality

Chapter 14: Releasing Attachments

Chapter 15: Release His Word

Chapter 16: God Deserve Our Obedience
Chapter 17: Nothing Should Separate Us

Chapter 18: Promised Outpouring of God Spirit)

Chapter 19: All Things Are Possible

Chapter 20: Giving Thanks in A Circumstances
Conclusion

Appendix A (Bibliography)

Introduction

My desire is to encourage the people of God to move forward in Him. The idea is to give you the fuel you need to get through the day. This devotion will encourage you, challenge you, and also give you the change you need in your life.

In the midst of writing this devotional book I have been encouraged, challenged, and changed. It allowed me to re-evaluate who I am in Christ and pushed me to start doing things correctly.

I do believe everyone will have a different experience while reading this devotion. Please take this One Day At A Time. The benefit is there, just reach for yours.

Be Blessed!

Dedication Page

This book is first dedicated to my Lord and Savior for giving me the idea to put this devotional together. Without His direction it would only be a thought.

The important thanks go to my best friend and wife Rhonda. We have been married for 20 years and have three wonderful children; Danielle (20), Kendra (19), and Isaac (16). They are such a joy. My wife always tells me, "Make sure you are hearing from God when you are trying to do something, so it can be effective when you present it to the people." It is because of her, and me truly consulting God on this project, that it took over three years to complete. When I would say, "the book is finished", she would say, "Have you added everything you needed to add?" Those words would make me revisit the book and add more. I just want to say honey, I Love You and thanks for your inspiration.

I also want to thank my Pastors Frank & Robin King. They have been very instrumental in helping me write this book. They challenge others to be an impact for the Kingdom. I believe this is one way I can impact the Kingdom.

Chapter 1

Training 4 Victory
"Philippians 3:12-14"

Within this scripture there are a couple of words I would like to define *Prize & Goal* for a better understanding of what Paul was trying to say through these scriptures.

Definition: Prize – Greek word: Disko which means striving and pressing on to a goal with intensity.

Definition: Goal – The mark set as a limit to a race. (Aim for the **Goal** with a purpose)

Paul said that his goal was to know Christ, to truly be like Him we need to know Him. To be all God wants us to be, we have to know who He is. The goal will take all our energy because it took all of Paul's energy. We shall not let anything distract us from focusing on our goals for Christ.

When we are training our mind we should lay aside everything that is harmful to us; this is anything that would keep us from reaching our goal.

"Take one minute and ask yourself this question"

- **What is holding you back from reaching your Goal?**

- **What can I do to strip this off? What is keeping me from reaching my Goal?**

If you are struggling with getting the answer for the last two questions, just continue to pray that God will reveal what you need to do to overcome those things that are keeping you from reaching your goal.

There are three primary keys to reaching your goals;

1. Finish Strong
2. Obtaining the Prize
3. Reward Presentation

As we look to reach each individual key, my prayer is that God will ignite something in our hearts to continue to press no matter how hard the training will be.

Finish Strong – Hebrew 12:1 (Read)

The huge crowd of witnesses' faithfulness is a constant encouragement to us, we do not struggle alone, and we are not the first to struggle with problems we face. There have been others who ran the race and won. This witness from them should stir our hearts to run and win with a strong finish. What an inspiring heritage we have in God.

If we plan to obtain a prize in the end we need to keep our eyes on the goal which is living for Jesus. When we loose sight of that, we find ourselves in an unstable position.

Obtaining the Prize – I Corinthians 9:24-27 (Read)

To get a better understanding of this topic we are going to define the word *Obtain* in the Greek & Webster dictionary.

Definition: Obtain – Greek word – "Tynakano" which means "Taking Part."

Webster defines it as – "To gain."

We have the opportunity through life to gain and take part in gaining the prize that God has for us once we have completed our assignment here on earth.

Winning a race requires focus and discipline; we have to know how we are going to accomplish our goal which is winning. Paul gives us a great illustration that helps us to understand this Christian walk takes hard work, dedication, self denial, and grueling preparation. This word grueling means; requiring extreme effort, we should spend every moment working on ourselves at a high octane level so we can get were we need to be in God.

Here are three essential disciplines to help us obtain our prize.

1. Prayer – The Bible says; pray without ceasing.

2. Bible Study – We have to study to show ourselves approved, so we can rightly divide the word of God.

3. Worship – We should worship him in Spirit & Truth.

Reward Presentation – II Timothy 4:7-8 (Read)

A Crown of Righteousness

- As he neared the end of his life, Paul could completely say he was faithful to the call of God on his life. The walk may not be easy but we need to stay faithful to the call that is on our life so we can be reward with the Crown of Righteousness. Here is a question for you to ponder;

"Are you Faithful to your call?"

Reflections

Explain your insight:

Chapter 2

No Competition
"I John 4:4"

We have to understand evil is stronger than we are in the natural. We can't fight the enemy in our own strength. We need to allow God to take over, He is stronger. When we allow God to take over, this is when we find ourselves overcoming temptation, just as Jesus did when he was in the wilderness. We need to get to a place when we are in our personal wilderness we can overcome temptation.

Overcoming Temptation – Matt 4:1-11 (Read)

When trying to tempt Jesus; Satan focused on the 3 P's. The enemy will use the same three P's to tempt us as well.

1. Physical needs & desires
2. Possessions & Power
3. Pride

Physical needs & desires – Matt 4:3,4 (Read)

Jesus was in the wilderness for forty days and forty nights. He was hungry because He consecrated himself before God with fasting. While in the wilderness the enemy did everything to get Jesus off focus by dangling the opportunity to turn rocks into bread so He could eat. Jesus chose not to loose sight of his purpose for bread. The reason for Jesus not using his divine power to satisfy His physical needs was to show us how to trust in Him. We need to push the plate away to get closer to God.

We need to remember many of our desires are normal and good, but God wants us to truly satisfy them in the right way and right time.

Possession & Power – Matt 4:5-7 (Read)

We have to understand that God isn't a magician; He will not perform upon our request. When the enemy came to tempt Jesus for the second time this is how Jesus replied; the word tells us not to put God to the test. For more on this scripture read Deut 6:16. The word is teaching us not to test the Lord or using His example to help us when the enemy is trying to test us with Possession & Power.

Pride – Matt 4:8-10 (Read)

It is interesting to see Satan trying to use something that doesn't belong to him. Today, the enemy offers us the world by trying to entice us with materialism and power. The reason the enemy does this is because he knows if this is not obtained in the right way it will cause a disruption in our lives. We have to remember the words Jesus said. You must worship the Lord your God and serve Him only. The word is here for us to use whenever the enemy tries a sneak attack on us. Amen!

Reflections

Explain your insight:

Chapter 3

Under New Management
"Galatians 5:1"

When looking at Christ in this verse it is a mark of the new dispensation. The word dispensation is from the Greek word "Oikonomia" which means "Management". We are living under a new management in Christ. Living under this management brings about an easy way of looking at who we are because of what the new management brings with Him (Jesus). Here are five marks of this New Management:

1. The mission to Proclaim Christ – Isaiah 61:1 **(Read)**
2. The Truth the Instrumentality – John 8:32 **(Read)**
3. A new law of life set free – Romans 8:2 **(Read)**
4. The Bondage of Sin Broken – Romans 8:21 **(Read)**
5. The Presence of the Spirit secures – 2 Corinthians 3:17 **(Read)**

We will engage each one for the next few minutes so we can get more understanding for our new management direction.

This mission of Christ to proclaim – Isaiah 61:1 (Read)

The mission of the New Management is:

- Bring Good News to the Poor
- Comfort the Brokenhearted
- Captives will be released
- Prisoners will be freed
- Mourners will experience the Favor of God

This is the mission of our Lord; we need to take on this assignment and see it through to completion.

The truth the Instrumentality – John 8:32 (Read)

Jesus is the truth we need to set us free. Here are several things Jesus will free us from:

- Consequences of Sin
- From self-deception
- From deception by Satan

These are things the enemy will use to keep us bound, but Jesus has come to set us free. If we allow Him to do it His way we will not have to worry about these things keeping us in bondage.

A new law of life set free – Romans 8:2 (Read)

The Holy Spirit is the life-giving Spirit we need to live in a place of freedom. The God we serve gives us the power to live in freedom everyday. How? By helping us understand who we are in Him. When we come to realize this information it makes it hard for the enemy to keep us bound.

The Bondage of Sin Broken – Romans 8:21 (Read)

When we allow sin to enter in, we allow our perfect state to be in jeopardy. There needs to be an understanding that Sin causes death and decay, so we will not be able to fulfill our intended purpose. There will be a day when liberation will come, so we can be transformed. We don't have to be entangled with the Yoke of Bondage any longer because we have a God who is willing to set us free (Galatians 5:1). Amen!

The Presence of the Spirit secures – II Corinthians 3:17 (Read)

God promises us freedom from…

- Sin – Romans 6:23 (Read)
- Condemnation – Romans 8:1 (Read)
- Old Mindset – Romans 8:6 (Read)

Where the Spirit of the Lord is there is Freedom.

Reflections

Explain your insight:

Chapter 4

Weathering the Storm
"Luke 8:25"

Definition: Weathering – "To come through (something) safely."

"To withstand the effects of weather."

Definition: Storm – "A heavy shower of objects, such as bullets or missiles."

The enemy is always trying to shower us with bullets of doubt and missiles of despair. There are times when the storm will rage. We have to learn how to withstand the effects of the weather and take shelter. The bible tells us. "He will hide us in the shadow of his wings". The key is learning how to take cover when we are showered with objects from the enemy. Here are a couple things we can look to when we are faced with doubt in the midst of the storm.

- We have to understand who we are in God. We are in relationship with a God who has already calmed the storm.

- We have to understand that God is all about our safety.

So, I have one question for you;

Where is your Faith?

It is easy to let the noise in around us and challenge our faith. The Lord is very sovereign when the storms of life try to take over; it is also our faith in God that keeps us grounded.

Reflections

Explain your insight:

Chapter 5

100% Guaranteed
"Numbers 23:19"

There is a 100% Guarantee with God. Why? Because God is…

1. Not a man, that he should lie.

   - If you look through the Bible you will find out how good God's track record is. God said it and it happened.

2. Not a human, that He changes his mind.

   - The mind of a human will change each day. The changing of our mind is something that is a part of our nature. We are faced with things that will challenge our mind on a daily basis. The thing about God is that His mind will never change.

3. He never fails to act.

   - When you call out to God for help, you can have this guaranteed that He will act upon what you ask Him for.

4. He promises and carries it through.

- The Lord promised us life. (John 10:10) Read

- The Lord promised us Financial Freedom. (Luke 6:38) Read

We can have confidence in Him. The information below will help us go deeper with this subject.

I. Sure Word – (Absolutely Trustworthy), sure.

A. Five basic prayer requests – I King 8:56-60 (Read)

1. For God's Presence.
2. For the desire to do God's will in everything
3. For the ability to obey God's decrees and commands
4. For help with each days needs.
5. For the spread of God's Kingdom to the entire world (City).

B. All he does is…. Psalms 111:7 (Read)

1. Just – Consistent with what is morally right.
2. Good – Reliable; Sure

3. Trustworthy – Taking responsibility for one's conduct and obligations.

II. Immutability – Will not change and always constant.

A. A never changing God – Hebrew 13:8 (Read)

1. Yesterday – He is awesome
2. Today – He is awesome
3. Forever – He is awesome

Nothing will ever change about God.

Reflections

Explain your insight:

Chapter 6

Walking In Confidence
"W.I.C"
"Hebrew 13:5-6"

"Those who Walk In Confidence, have the marks of a content person."[1]

Definition: Confidence –

- **Full Trust; belief in the power or reliability of a person or thing.**

Definition: Content –

- **Satisfied with what one is or has.**

We should have confidence in God knowing He will never leave us nor forsake us. We become content when we realize God's sufficiency is enough for our needs. People who want material things are saying that God can't do it like I can. The only antidote is to trust God to meet all our needs.

Definition: Antidote –

- **A remedy to counteract the effects of a person.**

When God says it, you can stake your life on it.

Three Areas of Confidence……

1. Gauging our Confidence Level.
2. Confidence vs. Arrogance!
3. What is your source of Confidence?

1. Gauging your Confidence Level

Definition: Gauging – **To determine the capacity or contents.**

A. Hebrew 10:35 (Read)

- God wants us to Trust Him, and confidence is the key.

- We can always gauge our confidence levels in God by asking ourselves this question:

"When adversity comes do I stand strong in the word, or do I immediately become frustrated and scared then cave in and quit?" Creflo Dollar

2. Confidence vs. Arrogance

Define: Arrogance – **One's own important.**

B. I Peter 5:5 (Read)

- Arrogant will keep us from going to another level in God, but confidence in Him will take us to the next level.

Humility is essential to our relationship with God. If we want to walk in God's grace (His unmerited favor) then we must lay aside our pride and be humble – not only to Him but also to one another.

Confidence and Pride are eternal enemies. Pride demands God to bless us in light of what we deserve. Confidence will only deal with us on the basis of what is in God, not on the basis of anything in us.

3. What is your source of Confidence?

Definition: Source – **A Supplier of Information**

"Can you trust God when circumstances make you apprehensive?"

Definition: Apprehensive – **Uneasy, Fearful about something that might happen.**

When I trust in God it gives me the calm confidence that it is not my abilities alone but in His trust and power.

Reflections

Explain your insight:

Chapter 7

The Love of Christ (TLC)
"Ephesians 3:18, 19"

Do you remember when you were a kid you had a crush on someone? We called that "puppy love?" This simply meant the love you had for that person was surface, it had nothing to stand on. True love gives you something to stand for. Puppy love is quick to change. It can be here today and gone tomorrow; a passing affection.

True Love is…..

- Unchangeable – John 13:1
- Divine – John 15:9
- Inseparable – Romans 8:35-39
- Compelling – II Corinthians 5:14
- Sacrificial – Galatians 2:20
- Manifested by His death – I John 3:16

These six things define what true love is all about, giving you a better understanding of His love.

A. Unchangeable – John 13:1 (Read Below)

Definition: Unchangeable – **Not changing**

Jesus knew He would be betrayed by one of His disciples, denied by another, and abandon by all but he still showed them what true love looks like. We are the same way, Jesus knows we are going to sin but he still loves us. The Love he has for us is in spite of what we do. Ask yourself this question.

"**How do you respond to this type of Love? (Think about this for a minute.)**

B. Divine – John 15:9 (Read)

Definition: Divine – **Eternal**

The Lord's desire is for us to remain in His love. It is amazing to know that Jesus loves us just as the Father loved Him.

C. Inseparable – Romans 8:35-39 (Read)

Definition: Inseparable – **Incapable of being separate**

Definition: Incapable – **Not open to**

We will go through so many hardships like persecution, illness, imprisonment, and even death. When we face these difficult things we sometimes feel like God has left us, but we can rest assure from these scriptures God's love for us is never separated from us. If we have confidence in His love we will never have to be afraid.

D. Compelling – 2 Corinthians 5:14

Definition: Compelling – **Attention or admiration powerfully irresistible way.**

Why is His love compelling (**irresistible**)?

- It controls us
- He died for us
- It gives us new life

The Love that Jesus has for us is irresistible because of how his spirit demands attention.

E. Sacrificial – Galatians 2:20 (Read)

Definition: Sacrificial - **Surrendering a possession**

How have we been crucified?

1. Legally – We died with Christ

2. Relationally – We are one with Christ
3. Daily Life – We must regularly crucify ourselves.

F. Manifested by His Death – I John 3:16 (Read)

Question…

Do you know what real love is?

How?

Christ gave His life for us. When He died for us His love was put into action. The way we put real love into action is by putting other people's desires before ours. Amen!

There is nothing that will keep us away from His true love.

Reflections

Explain your insight:

Chapter 8

Conflict between Flesh & Spirit
"Galatians 5:16-26"

In Greek the word conflict means adversaries or opponents; we all know living in God we are going to have specific opponents that are going to attack us right where we are. It is our understanding of those attacks that will get us through.

The enemy has a way of hiding what is from the flesh because he wants to get us to make a mistake. The Bible talks about wolves in sheep's clothing because this is the way the enemy can see (what he can slide in on us) as believers. This is why we always need to have spiritual antennas up to know what he is trying to do.

We all know there are two sides to every coin. We are hoping from this daily devotion you will determine which side of the coin you would like to be on. The way we are going to help is by looking at two pieces of the puzzle; which is flesh & spirit man. We will uncover from these two pieces, the **Sinful Nature (Mind) & Fruit of the Spirit (Characterized of God)**

Flesh Man:

Sinful Nature (Mind) – Galatians 5:16-18 (Read)

We will find ourselves doing things we are not suppose to do, this is because our mind is not on the right things. The flesh will always try to control everything. Rom. 1:28 (Read)

Does not submit to the Laws of God (Will of God)! Romans 8:7 (Read)

Controls how you think! Ephesians 4:17 (Read)

It will alienate you from God! Col. 1:21 (Read)

It is easy for the enemy to pick someone off that has alienated themselves from everyone else. The enemy uses the cares of life to separate us from his protection. When we decide to trust in God it gives us a sense of relief because we know that he will come through for us.

Sin Fruit – Galatians 5:19-21 (Read)

Here is a list of spoil fruit you do not want to be a part of:

A. Bitter – Jeremiah 2:19 (Read)
B. Sour – Isaiah 5:2 (Read)
C. **Selfish – Hosea 10:1 (Read)**

Spirit Man:

Spiritual Fruit – Galatians 5:22&23

Here is a list of good fruit that will help us grow:
1. Love
2. Joy
3. Peace
4. Patience
5. Kindness
6. Goodness
7. Faithfulness
8. Gentleness
9. Self-Control

A. Produced in all periods of life which means it will produce good fruit in every season. (Spring, Summer, Autumn, and Winter) Psalm 92:13&14 (Read)

B. It will grow only in good soil. Matt 13:8 (Read)
How does it grow in good soil?

1. **Contact with living water – Psalm 1:3 (Read0**
2. **Death of old life – John 12:24 (Read)**

3. **Chasten or Pruning – John 15:2 (Read)**
4. **Abiding in Christ – John 15: 5 (Read)**
5. **Protecting the soil from unwanted guest.**

C. **Many Varieties – Galatians 5:22&23 (Read)**
   - **Meditate on the variety of Fruit that grows inside of you.**

D. **Without Defect – Ephesians 5:9 & Philippians 1:11 (Read)**
   - **The right type of fruit growing on the inside of you has no defect. Why? It is produced by the Holy Spirit.**

We have looked at two different types of Fruit. According to Matt 7:20, what type of fruit are you producing? Is it sin or spirit! (Moment to reflect on that question)

Reflections

Explain your insight:

Chapter 9

Know the Truth/Rejecting the False
"I John 5:18-20"

These verses help us understand the true God, also to accept we are in His Son which helps us to be in God.

We are going to look at three absolute truths…"We Know"

1. Whoever is born of God does not sin.
   - I am not saying we are not tempted; we have help to keep ourselves from falling into sin.

2. That we are of God.
   - The reason we are of God, is because Christ resides on the inside of us.

3. The Son of God has come to give us understanding.
   - We now understand who we are and what our place is in the Kingdom. The enemy will do everything he can to tell us different.

The understanding we have from Christ enables us to know God in a personal and intimate way. If we can understand how this works, we will be in a position to go to another level.

Here is one question to think about....

What is Truth? Write your thoughts below.

Reflections

Explain your insight:

Chapter 10

B.I.G. = Believing In God
"Proverbs 3:5,6 & John 20:27"

Definition: Believe –
- **Put one's faith in or with implication that actions based on that truth may follow.**
- **To hold a firm connection; trust in.**

In Proverbs 3:5,6 it reminds us to *trust, lean,* and *acknowledge,* when that happens God will make our crooked path straight.

We all face seasons in our life where we have to *trust, lean, acknowledge* Him. It is my prayer that when you finish today's devotion your belief in God will grow to another level.

Why should you believe in God?

1. **Helps our Unbelief**
2. **It makes our connection with God Stronger**
3. **It helps us to hold on to our God said.**

Help our Unbelief

- The God we serve gives us everything we need, so he makes it easy for us to believe in Him. The enemy will do everything he can to destroy our faith in God but we need to Trust so our path can be straightened out.

It makes our connection with God stronger

- What I have learned from believing in God is looking at His track record and seeing that He has never failed us. When looking throughout the gospel, we find story after story of how He turned someone's life around. This alone should motivate us to trust God. I do understand life happens but God is the author of life.

It helps us to hold on to our God said

- There are things God has been saying to you, but the enemy will do everything he can to change what God is saying about you and your purpose. If you take a moment to remember your God said, it will strengthen your believe in God.

"What has God been saying to you?"

According to John 20:27; it took Thomas physically putting his finger in his hand in order for him to believe that Jesus was resurrected. If you think about it some of us are like Thomas, we have to physically see things before we believe. This doesn't mean you don't have faith in God, it means you just have to strengthen your faith.

How can we build our faith?

There are five ways to increase our faith.

1. Feed your Faith – II Thess. 1:3 (Read)

2. Love your brother – Galatians 5:6 (Read)

3. Fellowship with Him – Matt 18:20 (Read)

4. Act on your Faith – Mark 9:23 (Read)

5. Think on the word of God – Joshua 1:8 (Read)

If we take time to read and act on these scriptures, I do believe our faith will be charged in God. We have to encourage ourselves to believe in God no matter how we feel.

Here are some other scripture to help you believe in God.

- Psalm 37:3,5

- Psalm 118:8

- Isaiah 26:4

"Trust is the Key!"

Reflections

Explain your insight:

Chapter 11

Understanding the Love of Christ
"Luke 6:27&28, Ephesians 3:16-19, & Romans 5:8"

Today we will have an opportunity to reflect on four questions that will challenge your love walk. When reading these questions, answer them truthfully and honest.

1. **What would you do if someone falsely accused you, wronged you, and despitefully used you? Circle your answer**

    A. Get mad so you can get even?

    B. Get depressed and feel sorry for yourself?

    C. Bless and Pray for the one doing those things to you?

Ponder on this question and answer it to yourself.

2. How would you respond if someone asks something of you or from? Circle your answer

   A. Tell them to get their own for you work to hard for what you have.

   B. Make up an excuse that indicates to them you don't have what they are wanting or needs.

   C. Give them what they are asking for in Love and expecting no payment in return.

Ponder on this question and answer it to yourself.

3. How do you respond when you see an overweight/unattractive Christian? Circle your answer

   A. Do you immediately think if they truly love Jesus they would loose weight and get their hair done?
   B. Do you immediately pass judgment on their lifestyle, family upbringing, and their lack of self-control?

   C. Do you never notice such things and you get blessed by their smile

and how they carry themselves in God's Kingdom?

Ponder on this question and answer it to yourself.

4. How do you handle being adored, praised, and having good things done by others? Circle your answer

   A. Respond with kind words and love them right back.

   B. Pat yourself on the back for being the jolly good fellow you are.

   C. Say "Thank You" and immediately go find a mean selfish person to rub it in their face.

   D. Give all Glory to God.

Ponder on this question and answer it to yourself.

I understand when reading these questions, it was probably easy to answer them but, I tell you, some people struggle with answering these simple questions.

Why? Because there are some people who will handle these questions in the wrong way. My prayer is that everyone reading this devotion will always show the love of Christ.

Here are several scriptures to look at when it comes to understanding the love of Christ.

What is real love?

- Songs of Solomon – 8:6,7
- I Corinthians 13:13
- I John 3:16

These scriptures will also help clarify what real of love is.

Why is love so important? Jesus wanted us to know the commandments were given for two simple reasons.

1. To help us love God.

2. To Love others as we should.

What else did Jesus say about Love?

- **Matthew 5:43-48** *"You have heard that it was said, 'You shall love your neighbor and hate your enemy.' But I say to you, Love your enemies and pray for those who persecute you, so that you may be sons of your Father who is in heaven. For he makes his sun rise on the evil and on the good, and sends rain on the just and on the unjust. For if you love those* *who love you, what reward do you have? Do not even the tax collectors do the same? And if you greet only your brothers, what more are you doing than others? Do not even the Gentiles do the same? You therefore must be perfect, as your heavenly Father is perfect.*

- **Matthew 6:24-25** *"No one can serve two masters, for either he will hate the one and love the other, or he will be devoted to the one and despise the other. You cannot serve God and money. "Therefore I tell you, do not be anxious about your life, what you will eat or what you will drink, nor about your body, what you will put on. Is not life more than food, and the body more than clothing?*

- **Mark 12:28-30** *And one of the scribes came up and heard them disputing with one another, and seeing that he answered them well, asked him, "Which commandment is the most important of all?" Jesus answered, "The most important is, 'Hear, O Israel: The Lord our God, the Lord is one. And you shall love the Lord your God with all your heart and with all your soul and with all your mind and with all your strength.'*

- **John 14:21-24** *Whoever has my commandments and keeps them, he it is who loves me. And he who loves me will be loved by my Father, and I will love him and manifest myself to him." Judas (not Iscariot) said to him, "Lord, how is it that you will manifest yourself to us, and not to the world?" Jesus answered him, "If anyone loves me, he will keep my word, and my Father will love him, and we will come to him and make our home with him. Whoever does not love me does not* *keep my words. And the word that you hear is not mine but the Father's who sent me.*

- **John 15:9-17** *As the Father has loved me, so have I loved you. Abide in my love. If you keep my commandments, you will abide in my love, just as I have kept my Father's commandments and abide in his love. These things I have spoken to you, that my joy may be in you, and that your joy may be full. "This is my commandment, that you love one another as I have loved you. Greater love has no one than this, that someone lay down his life for his friends. You are my friends if you do what I command you. No longer do I call you servants, for the servant does not know what his master is doing; but I have called you friends, for all that I have heard from my Father I have made known to you. You did not choose me, but I chose you and appointed you that you should go and bear fruit and that your fruit should abide, so that whatever you ask the Father in my name, he may give it to you. These things I command you, so that you will love one another.*

Meditate on these scripture to help you understand real Love!

Reflections

Explain your insight:

Chapter 12

Seek First, Everything else second
"Matthew 6:33"

In Hebrew, the word seek means: to go after and to search for. In this life we have to search for the kingdom of God and His righteousness because this sets us up to receive everything else He (God) has for us. If we have no desire for the kingdom and His righteousness we will miss out on what God truly wants to release into our hands.

Over the next several minutes we will take a close look at the kingdom of God and His righteousness, we want to leave from this day with a better understanding of this scripture.

A. What does our text teach us?

Jesus comes to the **climax** of His argument. The kingdom is the ultimate focus for every believer.

But seek first the kingdom of God and His righteousness,

> ➢ The kingdom of God is more important than our personal agenda. The idea of the kingdom is the main subject of the Sermon on the Mount. The kingdom is to be our **controlling** priority.

- This verse picks up the same word for "seek" as in the last verse. "Seek" carries the idea of *concentrating on*, making the kingdom one's **highest priority**. "Seek" is in the imperative mood and calls for burning attention to the kingdom. The grammar also indicates a constant seeking. The idea is to "Make the kingdom the center of your life."

- The word "first" itself indicates **priority** and is emphatic in the sentence. We put kingdom issues above everything else. The idea is to put material things second. Believers are not to allow themselves to become distracted by personal needs from God's purpose for them.

- God's righteousness characterizes His kingdom. This is the **kind** of kingdom that believers are to pursue.

And all these things shall be added to you.

- "All these things" are material things. This refers to the Father knowing what we need in verse 32. The word "added" indicates that **God** will meet our needs as a matter of course. "These things" are the necessities of life. [2]

B. What do I want you to know?

1. **Nine results by seeking God, seeking God…**
   A. You will find him – Deuteronomy 4:29
   B. Regardless of life situation – 2 Chr 30:18-20
   C. Because he looks for you – Psalm 14:2
   D. With all your being – Psalm 63:1
   E. Before he has to get your attention – Psalm 78: 34
   F. He has arranged for you to do so – Acts 17:27-28
   G. Even when you don't feel like it – Romans 3:10-11
   H. He rewards you for it – Hebrew 11:6
   I. So you will know what to do – I King 22:5

We are going to take a closer look at these nine results to get a better understanding of what God is saying to us about seeking him…

A. You will find him – Deuteronomy 4:29

"^{29} But from there you will search again for the LORD your God. And if you search for him with all your heart and soul, you will find him."

➢ Search with all your heart.
➢ He wants to be known.
➢ Sincere devotion in the heart.

> Pursuing God brings rewards.

B. Regardless of life situation – 2 Chronicles 30:18-20

"[18] Most of those who came from Ephraim, Manasseh, Issachar, and Zebulun had not purified themselves. But King Hezekiah prayed for them, and they were allowed to eat the Passover meal anyway, even though this was contrary to the requirements of the Law. For Hezekiah said, "May the LORD, who is good, pardon those [19] who decide to follow the LORD, the God of their ancestors, even though they are not properly cleansed for the ceremony." [20] And the LORD listened to Hezekiah's prayer and healed the people."

> He will heal you.

C. Because he looks for you – Psalm 14:2

"2The LORD looks down from heaven
   on the entire human race;
he looks to see if anyone is truly wise,
   if anyone seeks God."

> Real Understanding.
> One who seeks for Him?

D. With all your being – Psalm 63:1

"O God, you are my God;
   I earnestly search for you.
My soul thirsts for you;
   my whole body longs for you
in this parched and weary land
   where there is no water."

- ➢ You are my God
- ➢ Earnestly search for Him
- ➢ My Soul Thirst
- ➢ Whole Body Long for Him

E. Before he has to get your attention – Psalm 78:34

"When God began killing them,
   they finally sought Him.
   They repented and took God seriously."

- ➢ We have to Repent & Turn to God

F. He has arranged for you to do so – Acts 17:27-28

"^{27} His purpose was for the nations to seek after God and perhaps feel their way toward him and find him—

though he is not far from any one of us. ²⁸ For in him we live and move and exist. As some of your[a] own poets have said, 'We are his offspring.'"

- God is known in His creation
- God is Transcendent
- God is creator
- God is sovereign
- God is in Control
- God is close & personal

G. Even when you don't feel like it – Romans 3:10-11

"¹⁰ As the Scriptures say,

"No one is righteous—
   not even one.
¹¹ No one is truly wise;
   no one is seeking God."

- No one is innocent
- No one is good
- No one can earn right standing with God
- He has redeemed us
- Everyone is valuable in God's eye because He created us in His image.

H. He rewards you for it – Hebrew 11:6

"⁶ And it is impossible to please God without faith. Anyone who wants to come to him must believe that God exists and that he rewards those who sincerely seek him."

➢ God assures us that all who honestly seek Him – who act in faith on the knowledge of God that they process – will be rewarded.

People should be flocking to Him – seeking Him – by the Multitudes, but they are not. Why?

1. Do they love the world and the things of the world too much? (I John 2:15,16)

2. Do they love the flesh and its feelings too much?

3. Do they love pride, fame, and power too much?

4. Do they just not know? Have they not heard? (Romans 10:14,15)

5. Are the witness and life of believers too weak? (Ephesians 4:17-24)[3]

Take a moment to answers these questions above in your mind to come to an understanding to why people are not seeking God.

Reflections

Explain your insight:

Chapter 13

True Holiness is Reality (The Way of Life)
"Hebrew 12:14"

"[13]Make every effort to live in peace with all men and to be holy; without holiness no one will see the Lord." (NIV)

The Greek word for True is "Alethinos" which mean Sincere. Are we sincere with our relationship to Jesus? The relationship Jesus is requiring from us should never come off as a fake.

A right relationship with God leads to right relationships with fellow believers. Although we will not always feel loving toward all other believers, we must pursue a genuine relationship the more we become Christ like. When I look at the word genuine, I define it as being **"free from Counterfeit."** We cannot live in a right relationship with God or man if we are not true to the relationship.

In order for our relationships to be real we need to walk in the spirit of Holiness. The word Holiness simply means to be **"Set Apart".** When we are set apart it puts us in a place of dedication to God. When we are dedicated to God, we are saying my devotion to God is selfless.

As we go through this day we will look at what being **"Set Apart"** means.

Set Apart means:

1. A Pure Heart – Matt 5:8

"The pure in heart — Those whose hearts are purified by faith; who are not only sprinkled from an evil conscience by the blood of Jesus, but cleansed by the Spirit of God from vain thoughts, unprofitable reasonings, earthly and sensual desires, and corrupt passions; who are purified from pride, self-will, discontent, impatience, anger, malice, envy, covetousness, ambition; whose hearts are circumcised to love the Lord their God with all their hearts, and their neighbours as themselves, and who, therefore, are not only upright before him, but possess and maintain purity of intention and of affection in all their designs, works, and enjoyments; serving him continually with a single eye and an undivided heart."[3]

We should always look for opportunity to have a pure heart. When we have this type of heart we are able to be sensitive to the Holy Spirit.

2. Maturity – II Corinthians 7:1

We need to understand that cleansing is a twofold action; they are turning away from sin and turning toward God. The Corinthians wanted to have nothing to do with sin, so they made a clean break from sin. I believe we should make a clean break from sin and give everything over to God.

3. Being Holy – I Peter 1:16

When we commit our lives to Christ, we sometimes feel a pull back to our old life. The Bible tells us to be like our heavenly Father which is to be Holy in everything we do. Holiness means being totally devoted or dedicated to God, set aside for his special use and set apart from the influence of sin. We need to understand that God qualities in our lives make us different from the world.

We cannot become holy on our own, but God gives us the Holy Spirit to help us obey and gain the power to over come the sins of the world.

4. Godly Lifestyle – II Peter 3:11

Should we spend more time piling up our possessions or striving to develop our Christ like character? We should always be striving to develop our character in God because it is what we have to sustain us in our lifestyle.

God is always looking for us to operate out of a lifestyle of Holiness, because this is how we get to the next level in God.

Reflections

Explain your insight:

Chapter 14

Releasing Attachments
"II Corinthians 5:17"

When we look at this word release it is define as "To relieve from something that oppresses, confines, or burdens,"

1. Oppresses – To weigh down
2. Confines – To keep within limits
3. Burdens – Cares of life

We define attachments as; a connection by which one or several things is attached to another. What have you attached to your life? Here are several plaques that have tried to attach to our lives.

A. Doubt
B. Fear
C. Disobedience
D. Jealousy (Envy)
E. Offense
F. Lust

These attachments are not good for us if we allow them to latch on to our lives and become a part of who we are as a person in God. At this time we are going to take a closer look at each attachment…..

A. Doubt – Make us vulnerable to temptation (Luke 4:3 NLT)

"Then the Devil said to him, "If you are the Son of God, change this stone into a loaf of Bread."(Luke 4:3 NLT)

The Webster dictionary defines doubt as *"a condition causing uncertainty, hesitation, or suspense."* When there is an uncertainty in our hearts about things it can put in a vulnerable position.

It was the scheme of Satan to get Christ to doubt his own identity. You see this when he uses the word "If" (**If you are the Son of God**) this word was put in this scripture to try and get Christ to question who he is; it is also used to get us to question who Christ is in our lives. It is far easier to get us to do what he wants when we doubt who Christ is to us.

B. Fear – Can immobilize you. (I Chronicles 28:20 NLT)

"Then David continued, Be Strong and courageous, and do the work. Don't be afraid or discouraged by the size of the task, the Lord God, my God is with you. He will not fail you are forsake you."

In this verse of Scripture David is looking to inform Solomon about the task at hand. The task was being a King and builder of the temple; it was at this time God told him not to be frightened by what he is supposed to be doing. Fear can immobilize us; Why? Because we look at the size of the job and its risk or the pressure of the situation and it can cause us to freeze and do nothing. We need not focus on the things that will immobilize us, but on getting the task finished.

> "The Hebrew word for fear is *Intimidate*." Why is Intimidate so important? It is because of the five words between **In** and **Date** which is *Timid* which means **lacking in courage or self-confidence**.

C. Disobedience – Makes our lives more difficult. (Deut. 2:14,15 NLT)

"So thirty-eight years passed from the time we first arrived at Kadesh-Barnea until we finally crossed Zered Brook. For the Lord had vowed this could not happen until all the men old enough to fight in battle had died in the wilderness. The Lord had lifted his hand against them until all of them had finally died."

The Webster dictionary defines Disobedience as one who refuses to obey. There are times in my life when I have refused to obey what is truth, and when I find myself doing this it truly makes my life difficult. We should always strive to be obedient to what God is trying to do in our lives.

In this verse of scripture God sentenced them to wandering in the wilderness because of their disobedience to his commands and rejected His love. We can find ourselves wandering in the wilderness because we choose to rebel against His authority and not heed to His command about living right. We often make our journey more difficult than necessary by disobedience. If we live according to His word, we will find our lives to be less complicated and more rewarding.

D. Jealousy (Envy) – Suspicious of a rival. (Genesis 13:7,8 NLT)

"So an argument broke out between the herdsmen of Abram and Lot. At that time Canaanites and Perizzites were also living in the land. Then Abram talked it over with Lot. This arguing between our herdsmen has got to stop, he said. After all, we are close relatives!"

The Greek word for Jealousy is (zelos) which is pronounced as {dzay'-los} which means desiring to have what someone else has. This spirit has destroyed people because of their envy of what other people may have in their life. Abram and Lot, herdsmen were arguing about petty stuff and not even focusing on the enemy they were facing. We as Christians are faced with the same thing, fighting with each other while the enemy is working. Here are three ways to fight against arguments…….

1. *Be trustworthy towards each other.*
2. *Stay focus on the goal at hand which is destroying the enemy.*
3. *Always stay love-centered.*

If you apply these three things to your life you will not allow Jealousy to come in because you are not focused on self.

E. Offense – Attack or Assault (Proverbs 17:9, and Proverbs 4:23)

"Disregarding another person's faults preserves love; telling about them separate close friends." Proverbs 17:9 NLT

Here is a question I would like for you to think about. **How do you defend against *Offense*?** Think about this for a moment. It's so easy to operate out of offense by spreading the hurt you feel at the point of attack. Here is the answer to this bold question. How do you defend against Offense?

1. Love –

In the above scripture you see disregarding another person's faults helps you to preserve your love for that person. It is not an easy thing to do when you have been done wrong but it is necessary to defend against this word that has killed so many people emotionally and spiritually.

2. Guard your Heart –

"Above all else, guard your heart, for it affects everything you do." Proverbs 4:23 NLT

Why is it such an important thing to guard your heart from the Spirit of Offense? I was reading this article by Michael Hyatt, within this article he gives three reasons we should guard our hearts.

Because your heart is extremely valuable. We don't guard worthless things. I take my garbage to the street every Wednesday night. It is picked up on Thursday morning. It sits on the sidewalk all night, completely unguarded. Why? Because it is worthless. Not so with your heart. It is the essence of who you are. It is your authentic self—the *core* of your being. It is where all your dreams, your desires, and your passions live. It is that part of you that connects with God and other people.

Because your heart is the source of everything you do. King Solomon says it is the "wellspring of life." In other words, it is the source of everything else in your life. Your heart overflows into thoughts, words, and actions.

In Tennessee, where I live, we have thousands and thousands of natural springs, where water flows to the surface of the earth from deep under the ground. It then accumulates in pools or runs off into creeks and streams.

If you plug up the spring, you stop the flow of water. If you poison the water, the flow becomes toxic. In either situation, you threaten life downstream. Everything depends on the condition of the spring.

Likewise, if your heart is unhealthy, it has an impact on everything else. It threatens your family, your friends, your ministry, your career, and, indeed, your legacy. It is, therefore, imperative that you guard it.

Because your heart is under constant attack. When Solomon says to guard your heart, he implies that you are living in a combat zone—one in which there are casualties.

Many of us are oblivious to the reality of this war. We have an enemy who is bent on our destruction. He not only opposes God, but he opposes everything that is aligned with Him—including us.[4]

According to the article we can't take guarding our hearts lightly. The enemy is doing everything he can to destroy us in every possible way.

F. Lust – How it is very harmful. Colossians 3:5

*"So put to death the sinful, earthly things lurking within you. Have nothing to do with sexual sin, impurity, **lust**, and shameful desires. Don't be greedy for the good things of this life, for it is Idolatry."* NLT

We define this word in the *Greek* as (*pathos*) which means a **Strong Desire;** we are faced with this each day. When you are in a mindset of wanting something so bad you will do anything to fulfill the desire.

Here are some scripture references to help you counter attack this word ***Lust***.

1. Proverbs 25:28
2. Romans 6:12
3. Galatians 5:24
4. I Thessalonians 5:8
5. Titus 2:6

These attachments can kill, so release them from your life. Take a few minutes to reflect and write down some personal notes below.

Reflections

Explain your insight:

Chapter 15

Release His Word
"Proverbs 18:21"

This day is going to be different from the rest. Today will be for you to speak the word over your life. How awesome it is to wake up and begin to speak His word over your life. The best way I know how to end these fifteen days is to use the word to speak life into our spirits. There are fifteen days to this devotional book, so the right way to end this is to have 15 high octane scripture to speak into your life.

There are going to be several titles we will look at when it comes to using the scripture to speak over us. The topics are:

1. Favor
2. Strength
3. Finance

When reading these verses of scriptures; read them with a sense of seeing the manifestation of God's word.

1. Favor

- *For the Lord God is a sun and shield; the Lord bestows favor and honor. No good thing does he withhold from those who walk uprightly. (Psalm 84:11 ESV)*

- *Therefore do not be anxious, saying, 'What shall we eat?' or 'What shall we drink?' or 'What shall we wear?' For the Gentiles seek after all these things, and your heavenly Father knows that you need them all. But seek first the kingdom of God and his righteousness, and all these things will be added to you. (Matt 6:31-33 ESV)*

- *May the God of hope fill you with all joy and peace in believing, so that by the power of the Holy Spirit you may abound in hope? (Romans 15:13 ESV)*

- *This Book of the Law shall not depart from your mouth, but you shall meditate on it day and night, so that you may be careful to do according to all that is written in it. For then you will make your way prosperous, and then you will have good success. (Joshua 1:8 ESV)*

- *He who dwells in the shelter of the Most High will abide in the shadow of the Almighty. I will say to the Lord, "My refuge and my fortress, my God, in whom I trust." For he will deliver you from the snare of the fowler and from the deadly pestilence. He will cover you with his pinions, and under his wings you will find refuge; his faithfulness is a shield and buckler. (Psalm 91:1-4 ESV)*

"When quoting these scriptures understanding is that God will give His favor, all you have to do is ask."

2. Strength

- *Fear not, for I am with you; be not dismayed, for I am your God; I will strengthen you, I will help you, I will uphold you with my righteous right hand. (Isa. 41:10)*

- *The LORD is my strength and my song, and he has become my salvation; this is my God, and I will praise him, my father's God, and I will exalt him. (Exodus 15:2)*

- *The God who equipped me with strength and made my way blameless. He made my feet like the feet of a deer and set me secure on the heights. He trains my hands for war, so that my arms can bend a bow of bronze. (Psalm 18:32-34)*

- *I can do all things through him who strengthens me. (Philippians 4:13)*

- *No temptation has overtaken you that is not common to man. God is faithful, and he will not let you be tempted beyond your ability, but with the temptation he will also provide the way of escape, that you may be able to endure it. (I Corinthians 10:13)*

We tend to find ourselves needing God strength. When you are feeling like you have no strength to move on please remember to rehearse these scriptures on Strength, he will give you the shot you need to endure.

3. Finance

- *The Lord shall increase you more and more, you and your children. (Psalm 115:14 KJV)*

- *The Lord will grant you abundant prosperity – in the fruit of your womb, the young of your livestock and the crops of your ground – in the land he swore to your ancestors to give you. The Lord will open the heavens, the storehouse of his bounty, to send rain on your land in season and to bless all the work of your hands. You will lend to many nations but will borrow from none. The Lord will make you the head, not the tail. If you pay attention to the commands of the Lord your God I give you this day and carefully follow them, you will always be at the top, never at the bottom. (Deuteronomy 28:11-13 NIV)*

- *And my God will supply every need of yours according to his riches in glory in Christ Jesus. (Philippians 4:19 ESV)*

- *Whoever can be trusted with little can also be trusted with much, and whoever is dishonest with very little will also be dishonest with much. (Luke 16:10)*

- *Give and it will be given to you: A good measure, pressed down, shaken together, running over, will be poured into your lap. For the measure you use will be the measure you receive. (Luke 6:38 NET)*

Our finances are important to God so let's honor him with what we have so he can release more into our hands so we can experience the financial freedom we deserve because of who we are in Christ.

We've come to our last reflection. What I am going to ask you to do with this reflection is to pick out five scriptures from Favor, Strength, and Finances. Next, write down your understanding of those scriptures. This will give you something to look back on when encouragement is needed.

Reflections

Explain your insight:

Chapter 16

God Deserve Our Obedience
"Exodus 4:18-31"

The Definition of Deserve is a simple one which means; **"To Be Worthy of,"** this is to inform you that God is worthy of our obedience to Him.

1. Why do God deserve our Obedience?

A. The Rock of Character – (Matthew 7:24 NLT)

"To build on solid rock means to be a hearing, responding disciple, not a phony, superficial one. Practicing obedience become the solid foundation to weather the storms of life," *James 1:22-27* has a more on putting into practice what we hear.

B. Essential to Membership in God's Family – (Matthew 12:50 NLT)

"If you are not in true relationship with God, you will find yourself outside the family. It is our obedience to God that gives us membership into God's family."

C. The Key to Spiritual Knowledge – (John 7:16-18 NLT)

"Those who attempt to know God's will and do it will know that Jesus was telling the truth about himself. Have you ever listened to religious speakers and wonder if they were telling the truth?" Test them. How?

- Their words should agree with, not contradict the Bible.
- Their words should point to God and his will, not to themselves.

D. Secures the Blessings of Divine Fellowship – (John 14:23 NLT)

"Not everyone could understand Jesus' message. Ever since Pentecost the Good News of the Kingdom has been proclaimed in the whole world, and yet not everyone is receptive to it. Jesus saves the deepest revelations of himself for those who love and obey him.

2. What is the Requirement for Obedience

A. Wholehearted – (Deut. 26:16 & Deut. 32:46 NLT)

- According to Deut. 26:16, God is calling us to Obedience without any reservation or resistance.
- According to Deut. 32:46, Moses urged the people to think about God's word and teach it to their children.

"The Bible can sit on your bookshelf and gather dust or you can make it a vital part of your life by regularly setting aside time to study. When you discover the wisdom of God's message this will give you the opportunity to apply it to your life. This will also give you the opportunity to pass it on to your family and friends. The Bible is not merely a good read but its real help for real life."

B. The Price of Success – (Joshua 1:8 NLT)

- "Many People think prosperity and success comes from having power, influential personal contact, and a relentless desire to get ahead. The strategy for gaining prosperity that God taught Joshua goes against our criteria." He said to succeed we must:

    1. Be Strong and Courageous because the task at hand would not be easy.
    2. Obey God's Law.

3. Constantly read and study the Word of God.

- "To be successful we must follow God's word told to Joshua. You may not succeed by the world's standard but you will succeed in God's Eyes and His opinion lasts forever."

Obedience is our success to the Kingdom of God, without it we will not have much success. We need to always remember Obedience is Key.

Reflections

Explain your insight:

Chapter 17

Nothing Should Separate Us
"Romans 8:35-39"

"Paul is talking to the Romans about not letting the things of the enemy separate them from the Love of God. The first thing we have to understand is, we should be inseparable from God." Here is what it means:

I. Being inseparable from God. (Believers are constantly)

A. Accompanied by His Presence – Matthew 28:20 NLT
B. Held close by His Hand – John 10:28 NLT
C. Like Branches on the Vine – John 15:4 NLT
D. In Perpetual Fellowship – John 17:23 NLT
E. No Power or Darkness can Separate us – Romans 8:38 & 39

A. Accompanied by His presence – (Matthew 28:20 NLT)

"How is Jesus with us? Jesus was with the disciples physically until he ascended into heaven and then spiritually through the Holy Spirit (Acts 1:4 NLT). The Holy Spirit would be Jesus presence that would never leave Him (them) (John 14:26 NLT). Jesus continues to be with us today through his Spirit."

B. Held close by His Hand – (John 10:28 NLT)

"Just as a Shepherd protect his sheep; Jesus protects his people from eternal harm. While believers can expect to suffer on earth, Satan cannot harm our souls or take away our eternal life with God. There are many reason to be afraid here on earth because this is the Devil's playground (I Peter 5:8 NLT). But if we choose to follow Jesus, He will give us everlasting safety.

C. Branches on the Vine – (John 15:4 NLT)

"We are able to bear must fruit because we are inseparable from God. The fruit is good fruit, people are able to eat from the table, when it is connected to the vine."

D. In Perpetual Fellowship – (John 17:23 NLT)

"The Definition of Perpetual is Permanent or Continuous. The way I see it; is our fellowship with Jesus is not only continuous but it is Permanent. There are times in live we think our fellowship with God is on a Temporary bases but in his eyes, He sees a long lasting relationship with the people who have a heart for him."

E. No Power or Darkness can separate us – (Romans 8:38 & 39 NLT)

"Power are unseen forces of evil in the universe, forces like Satan and his fallen angels (Ephesians 6:12 NLT). In Christ we are super-conquerors, and His love will protect us from any such forces."

Reflections

Explain your insight:

Chapter 18

Promised Outpouring of God (Spirit)
"Isaiah 32:15 & Ezekiel 39:29"

The word Outpouring is a Hebrew word which means to pour out or Spill out, I am looking forward to God Spirit just spilling out all over us.

1. Five Areas that God promised an outpouring of His Spirit:

A. Upon Young and Old – (Joel 2:28 NLT)

"The Outpouring of the Spirit and the ministries done through His power will be accomplished without regard to gender, age, or class."

B. Christ the Giver of – (Matt 3:11 NLT)

"He Baptize you with the Holy Spirit; John identified people with himself and his message of repentance by water baptism; the one coming after him was so greater that He would unite people to Himself by means of the Holy Spirit. John knew the Kingdom to come would be characterized by the great display of the Holy Spirit in the lives of His people."

C. Bestowed in Answered Prayer – (Luke 11:13 NLT)

"How much more will your heavenly father give: If people, who are evil can give good gifts imagine the value of God's gift of the Holy Spirit. If anyone does not have the Holy Spirit, that person does not belong to Christ (See Romans 8:9 NLT). In the Triune Godhead the Holy Spirit is the divine distributor (See I Corinthians 12:11 NLT) of good things purchased by the Son (See Ephesians 4:7,8 NLT) and ordained by the father."

D. Through Waiting Upon God – (Luke 24:49 NLT)

"Promise of My father: This is a reference to the baptism of the Holy Spirit at Pentecost (See Acts 2). It was promised in Joel 2:28 (See Acts 2:14-18 NLT, and in Jeremiah 31:31-33 NLT). Peter called this coming of the Spirit "the beginning" (See Acts 11:15 NLT) because the real fulfillment of God's promise of Salvation. Tarry in the City of Jerusalem until you are endued with power from on High; The Disciples were to remain in Jerusalem until the Spirit empowered them on the day of Pentacost."

E. Empowered for Service – (Acts 1:8 NLT)

"Instead of being concerned about the date of Christ's return, the disciples' job was to carry His message throughout the world."

"God has promised us an outpouring of his Spirit; we need to prepare ourselves to receive that promise."

Reflections

Explain your insight:

Chapter 19

All Things Are Possible!
"Matthew 19:26"

"Jesus looked at them intently and said, humanly speaking, it is impossible. But with God everything is possible. NLT"

- The Word tells us humanly speaking it is impossible. Which means there are limitations to our human ability.

1. Three possible things with God. (Study All Three Scripture)

A. Sound Mind – 2 Timothy 1:7

"For God has not given us a spirit of fear, but of power and of love and of a sound mind." (NKJV)

B. Victory – I Corinthians 15:57

"But thank God! He gives us victory over sin and death through our Lord Jesus Christ." (NLT)

C. Freedom – Psalms 34:19

> "The righteous person faces many troubles,
>   but the LORD comes to the rescue each time."
> (NLT)

"Our faith grows stronger when we come to realize that with God everything is possible. These scripture are showing us how all things are possible with God."

Reflections

Explain your insight:

Chapter 20

Giving Thanks in All Circumstances
"I Thessalonians 5:18"

"Giving Thanks in all circumstances; for this is the will of God in Christ Jesus for you." NIV

"Therefore, we should develop the attitude of thanksgiving in Obedience to God."

The Definition of gratitude is readiness to show appreciation. We should always remember to very appreciative to what God is doing for us every day. Are you ready to appreciate what God has done for you? Are you ready to let him know how you are committed to Him?

A. Here are several principles to remember about Thankfulness.

1. Enter His Gates – Psalms 100:4 NLT

> "We should always come to him with thanksgiving in our hearts. It is when we are truly thankful that God extends his hand to us so He can release more."

2. Come before His presence – Psalms 95:2 NLT

> "Our duty when we come before God is to be thankful to Him. This is our opportunity to let Him know how much we appreciate Him for all He does for us."

3. Due His Righteousness – Psalms 7:17 NLT

- Definition of Righteousness in Greek is **Dikaiosune** which means the condition acceptable to God.

> "The Principle is design to help you understand how acceptable you are to God; He truly sees pass our flaws and looks at our heart. God truly sees us through the eyes of Grace."

4. Not being Anxious about anything – Philippians 4:6 NLT

- Definition of Anxious in the Greek is **Merimnao** which means concerned or worried.

> "It is not our job to worry about anything, but God is asking us to pray about everything. It is prayer that gets us through everything; when we pray we are making our request known to Him; and it is out of our time with Him, we should be thankful for what He has done and preparing to do."

   5. Everything comes from you – I Chronicles 29:12-14 NLT

- What comes from God?
    a. Wealth
    b. Honor
    c. Strength
    d. Power

- What comes from us?
    a. Thanks
    b. Praise

Our God is awesome; he gives us so much more even when we give little. Continue to remember these principles as you go through life.

Reflections

Explain your insight:

Conclusion

"After reading this book, my hope is that you will find renewed strength in your walk with God. What I have learned is our walk with God is **One Day At A Time**.

This is God's design and ideal for us to be lifted up. I hope you were encouraged and strengthened by the words from this book. Be Blessed!"

Appendix A

Bibliography

1. Standatthecrossroads.com – "Walking in the confidence of God", unknown author

2. Verse by Verse Commentary by Dr. Grant C Richardson; page unknown

3. Practical Word Studies in the New Testament; A-K Volume 1

4. Your Virtuous Mentor "Win at Work, Success at Life Article by Michael Hyatt

Scripture & Commentary by Life Application Study Bible (NLT) Tyndale

Made in the USA
Columbia, SC
20 December 2024